W9-BVN-115

AGING LIKE A FINE WHINER

Maxine's Guide to Birthdays

Illustrated by *J. Wagner*

Copyright © 1997 Hallmark Cards, Inc.

All rights reserved, including the right to reproduce this book
or any portions of this book. For information, contact:
Hallmark Cards, Inc., Kansas City, MO 64141

Published in the United States of America
by Hallmark Cards, Inc.

ISBN: 0-87529-716-1

Made in China.

5

You know you're old when you come down with illnesses that haven't been around in 40 years.
No, Doc, it's not the vapors. It's more like the conniptions.

There are a few disadvantages to aging... For instance, some of the shock value of mooning is lost when you have to explain what exactly the moonee is looking at.

20

A birthday
 is a good time
to salute Father Time.
Which finger
 you salute him with
is your business.

25

Birthdays
are like kicks in the butt...
a lot more fun
when somebody else
is on the receiving end.

30

Another birthday is nothing to sneeze at.
Right. At my age I could easily blow out some teeth.

Aren't birthdays fun?
Oh, yeah...
And you know
what else is fun?
Getting a potato chip
stuck between your
front teeth, so when you try
to get it out with your tongue,
you slice both your tongue
and your gum.
That's a real hoot.

OK if I give the birthday person a little kiss?
Do you really want that to be the last thing you do before losing consciousness?

You're not getting older,
you're getting better!
And you're not getting stupider,
you're getting...
hey, wait a minute!
You ARE getting stupider!

Well, you're still looking spry for your age.
Only if spry means I can still take you down and sit on you.
47

Part 3: *Maxine's* Birthday Quiz for the Chronologically Challenged

Which phone number does NOT belong on an older person's speed-dial?

    a) A doctor
    b) Another kind of doctor
    c) Yet another doctor
    d) A ski resort

(Answer: Trick question! They **all** belong!
The ski resort is where you can track down your doctor.)

Which craft is most popular among older people?
a) Gluing colorful rocks to stuff.
b) Crocheting things to put on furniture.
c) Gluing colorful rocks to things you've crocheted.

Unscramble the letters to find the word older people use most.

"UHH?"

(Answer: "Huh?")

Complete this phrase: It may be a sign you're getting older when...

a)...you buy your gas at the "Full Serve" island.
b)...the attendant at the "Full Serve" island gives you your very own rest room key.
c)...the attendant at the "Full Serve" island rudely returns to his job after 15 minutes of nodding at your weather observations.

Are you really old? Take this quiz:

a) Your parents came to America because they were "fed up with the King."
b) You still fear that the TV may be able to see you.
c) You believe that horses are still the most reliable transportation.

(Answer: If you answered, "Quit flappin' yer gums, ya whippersnapper!" you are officially old.)

56

Unsightly wrinkles and age spots can be camouflaged by:
a) An inch-thick covering of cold cream.
b) A pair of those comically big sunglasses.
c) A quick, sharp poke in the eyes of anyone who looks at you.
?